The Body Is Round

by

Linda C. Ehrlich

The Body Is Round
by
Linda C. Ehrlich

Copyright © 2015 by Shika Press Ltd.
All rights reserved.

ISBN 9780985878665

Published by Shika Press Ltd.

Shaker Heights, Ohio, USA

What stories do our hands tell?

Gestures from around the world.

To move and be moved

we dance…

...entranced

      by sound.

To heal the Earth

We offer...

...our hand

through time,

circling

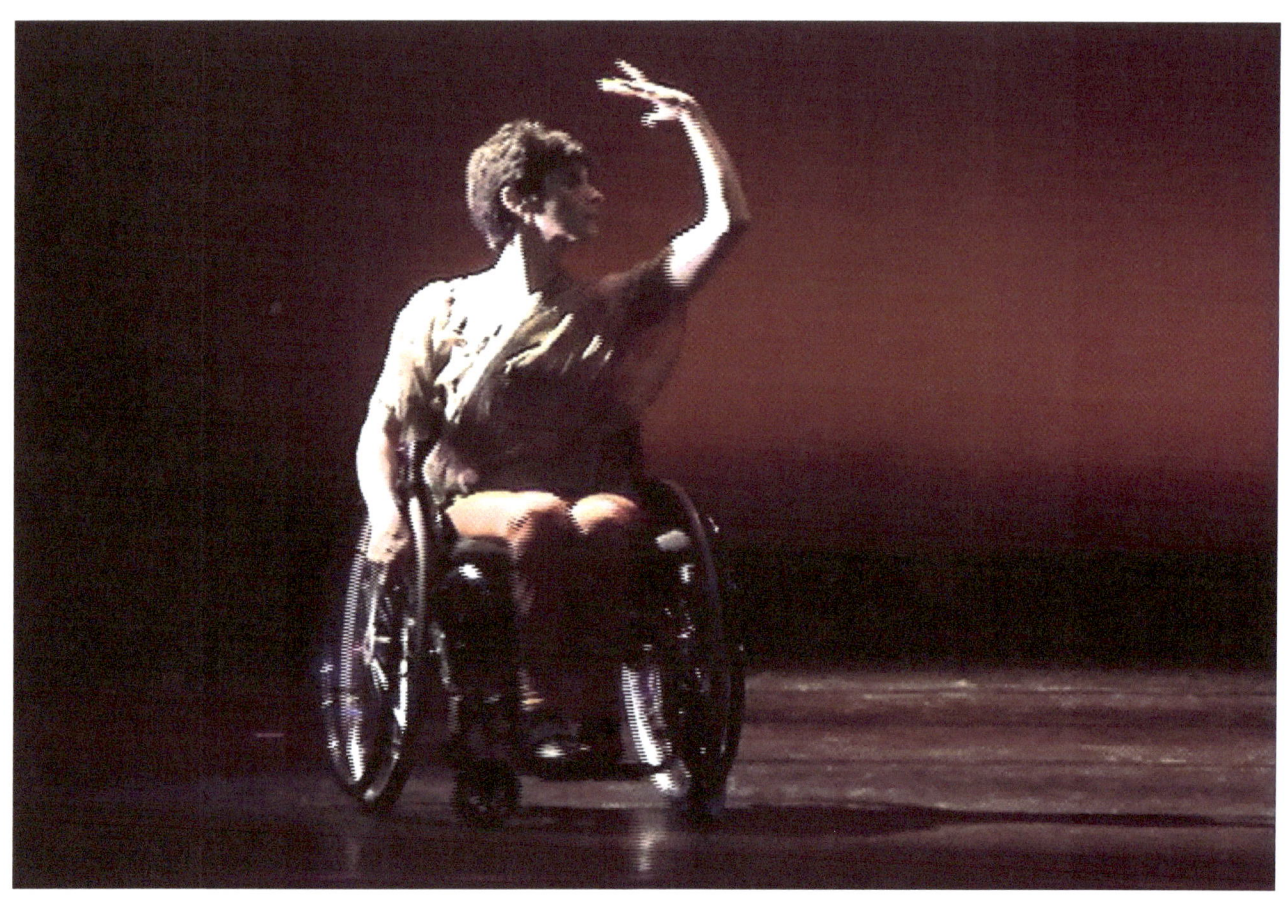

wheels within wheels.

We dance...

...because the body is round.

To move and be moved

we dance

entranced by sound.

*To heal the Earth
we offer our hand
through time,*

*circling
wheels within
wheels.*

*We dance
because the body is round.*

More About the Pictures

p. 1

The Hindu god Shiva dances destruction (fire in the upper left hand), and creation (drum in the upper right hand), surrounded by the rhythm of the Universe (circle of flames).

In the crown, a crescent moon. A skull and the goddess *Gunga*, the river Ganges, are entwined in the dancer's hair.

Underfoot, a small figure of Illusion is stamped into silence. And all the while, *Shiva Nataraj* dances endless cycles, eternally still, eternally in motion.

p. 3

In *Bharata Natyam,* a devotional dance from India, the dancers wear colorful costumes with elaborate jewelry. This dance form combines *bhava* (expression), *raga* (musical modes), and *tala* (rhythm). Bells around the dancer's feet add to the percussive effect.

The bride's dance beckons in the husband as if he were a god. With her hands she spells out her happiness, circling her face with a *mudra* (gesture) like the moon. Krishna, her shining groom with a face the color of the clear blue sky.

p.5

We learn about the great Khmer Kingdom of Angkor (802-1431) through stone carvings of *apsaras* (carved celestial dancers) on the crumbling walls of temples in banyan forests. The dancer opens her hands like the petals of a lotus flower in bloom, stretching them back into an impossible angle.

But the Khmer Rouge takeover of the government in 1975 destroyed dance schools and forbade the teaching of the classical dances at pain of death. Still the dance was hidden in the bones of the teachers. Since 1979, there has been a resurgence of traditional dances based on Hindu-Buddhist mythology. Dancers soothe their country's nightmares with a shimmering hand.

p. 6-7

Mad Hot Ballroom traces the course of ballroom dance classes at 3 elementary schools in the New York City area in preparation for a dance competition. 11-year-old kids with rhythm and lots to say. Boys who have been hanging around street corners tuck in their shirt tails. Girls who have been sassing their parents learn how to follow with clear-cut grace.

The one with the shy, angelic face who has recently arrived in this country. When he dances, he is the rumba itself with all its smoothness and grace.

Proud parents watch from the sidelines but the kids have already moved on. As the judges watch, and their friends cheer from below, the kids dance their hearts out.

p. 9
Ellis Island of the large drafty halls. Perched outside of New York City, this doorway to a new country. Tired travelers who have crossed the ocean await the moment when they can walk out into the light. Waiting, the immigrants take a moment to dance to songs transplanted in the new world. Uncertain of the future, still they dance.

Lewis Hine (1874-1940), factory worker turned photographer, went to Ellis Island in 1904 to record new immigrants who passed through the doors of this way-station into a land they hoped would hold promise. With a simple camera on a tripod he took one exposure. One chance was all he had. One chance, if they were lucky, was all they had as well.

p. 11
Shakers, a religious community who dared to live together in peace, men and women equally valued. "Hands to work and hearts to God." At one point they had 19 communities and they grew only by attracting new members inspired by their way of life.

After the dinner meeting—and as part of prayers—they would gather, men in one group, women in another, under the soft light of oil lanterns.
Older women instructed the small children. The whooshing of the long skirts on their plain woolen dresses echoed the hardwood floor.

Simple gifts of sun and air. Forward, backward, and around and around. At times they held their hands with palms upraised as if holding water from a
precious spring.

Traces of the Shakers are now echoed in a song by American composer Aaron Copland, and in a choreography by a modern dancer inspired by their vision. In Doris Humphrey's *The Shakers* (1931), we find Revelations, ecstatic hops, a weighted walk, a lengthening breath.

p. 12-13

The dancer in the wheelchair spins in circles, her arms extended. She carries the dance in her hands, tracing arcs along the floor. The spokes are like drumbeats; the spaces between the spokes, moments of rest. The rim is the melody circling around.

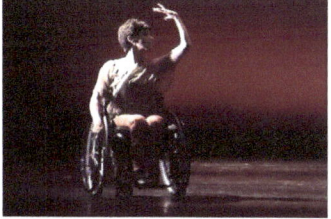

The chair helps all the dancers achieve something very new, very fast. Grab the hand of a sit-down dancer and feel how powerfully you can move through space.

p. 17

La Sardana, circles within circles, short and long steps. This dance from Catalonia (Spain) is accompanied by an 11-person *cobla* (band) of horns, drums and *cornamusa* (bagpipe). Men and women of all ages join together in the square in front of Barcelona's Cathedral, right in the middle of the city, or in the plaza of a small town. Suddenly the people join hands, raise their arms, and the *sardana* begins.

Anyone can join who knows the dance.

p. 19

Bedhaya is a Javanese refined court dance where nine young women move in unison, no one standing out more than the others. Dressed in elegant *batik sarongs,* accompanied by a *gamelon* orchestra of gongs and drums, the women move as if goddesses of the sea under the water. Their feet trace a precise and intricate *mandala*-like pattern on the floor.

This slow, stylized dance is a *pusaka*, a royal heirloom, a jewel of equilibrium and grace.

p. 21

The dancers of the *Mochibana* ("rice cake flower") dance carry pink and yellow flowers as they chant and pound out the rhythm with their fans. Wakanoura (Waka Bay) is on the coast south of the city of Wakayama (Japan).

"Solid, ironical, rolling orb!" (Walt Whitman)

The world irreplaceable
joins in the dance.

ACKNOWLEDGEMENTS

Invaluable technical assistance was provided by the CWRU Freedman Center, with a special thanks to Jared Bendis and Corey Wright. Corey's excellent eye for images greatly enhanced the book design.

The world of Shaker dance was opened up to me thanks to the generosity of the curators of the Shaker Historical Society and Museum.

Special thanks to the artists who appear in the illustrations. This book is dedicated to dance teachers and partners, and in memory of Alan and Cynthia.

ILLUSTRATIONS

Cover - Groundworks Dance Theatre (2007), David Shimotakahara, Artistic Director. Photo by Dale Dong.

1 *Nataraj, Shiva as the King of Dance*, South India, Chola period, 11th century, bronze, courtesy of the Cleveland Museum of Art, J.H. Wade Fund 1930.33.

3 *Le fleuve* (*The River,* 1951, India/France, directed by Jean Renoir, based on a novel by Rumer Godden). Courtesy of Janus Films.

5 *The Tenth Dancer* (photo by Ponch Hawkes), directed by Sally Ingleton, courtesy of Women Make Movies.

6-7 *Mad Hot Ballroom* (2005, U.S., directed by Marilyn Agrelo, produced by Amy Sewell).

9 Hine, Lewis, ¨Immigrants detained at Ellis Island take time to be happy,¨ in ¨Ellis Island¨ series, 1905, gelatin silver print, Gift of the Photo League, New York, ex-collection of Lewis Wickes Hine. Courtesy of the George Eastman House.

11 *Shakers at Meeting: The Religious Dance,* wood engraving, from *The Graphic* (May 14, 1870), courtesy of the Shaker Historical Society and Museum, Shaker Heights, Ohio.

12 *Dead Can Dance.* Choreography by Sabatino Verlezza. Frame grab courtesy of James Hacha (2003).

13 *Equilibria.* Choreography by Sabatino Verlezza. (2002). Image courtesy of Tracy Pattison.

17 Personal photo, Barcelona, Spain. (2002)

19 *Bedhaya* (Javanese court dance) From *Dancing: Dance at Court* (Thirteen/WNET in association with RM Arts and BBC-TV, 1993).

21 (Anonymous) ¨Rice Pounding Dance at Wakanoura¨ (detail), Japan, first half 19th century. Courtesy of the Spencer Collection, New York Public Library, Astor, Lenox and Tilden Foundations.

35 Personal photo, Louisville, Kentucky, 1960's.

www.ingramcontent.com/pod-product-compliance
Lightning Source LLC
Chambersburg PA
CBHW041119300426
44112CB00002B/30